Published in paperback in 2020 by Wayland
Copyright © Hodder and Stoughton, 2018

Wayland, an imprint of
Hachette Children's Group
Part of Hodder and Stoughton
Carmelite House
50 Victoria Embankment
London EC4Y 0DZ

Managing editor: Victoria Brooker
Creative design: Paul Cherrill

ISBN: 978 1 5263 0591 6

Printed in Dubai

FSC
www.fsc.org
MIX
Paper from
responsible sources
FSC® C104740

An Hachette UK Company
www.hachette.co.uk
www.hachettechildrens

INCREDIBLE RAINFORESTS

Written by
Kay Barnham

Illustrated by
Maddie Frost

WAYLAND

Did you know that most rainforests
are near the equator?
This is an imaginary line that runs
around the middle of Earth.

The equator is closer to the Sun than any other part of our planet. Here, the weather is very hot. In rainforests, it is also very wet.

A rainforest has four layers. At the top, giant trees reach towards the sky. Below, more treetops form the forest roof. This is where most animals live.

Shrubs and bushes grow in the shade beneath the trees. At the bottom, there is the forest floor, where few plants grow.

Plant leaves take in a gas called carbon dioxide.
Then they give out another gas called oxygen.
Humans breathe oxygen.

There are so many plants in rainforests that nearly half of the world's oxygen comes from here. This means that rainforests are important for all living creatures.

Rainforests have their very own water cycle. It is so hot that water vapour rises from the rainforest's plants. Clouds form above the rainforest.

When it rains, the thick forest roof catches the raindrops. Then hot weather makes water vapour rise all over again.

Even though rainforests only cover
a small part of our planet, they are
home to many, many living things.

Two out of every three types of plant grow in rainforests. Half of all animal species live in rainforests too. New species are being found all the time.

Plants need light to grow. In a rainforest,
trees grow very tall so that the Sun
can shine on them.

Vines climb up the trees to reach the sunlight at the top of the rainforest. Orchids and many other plants grow among the high branches, too.

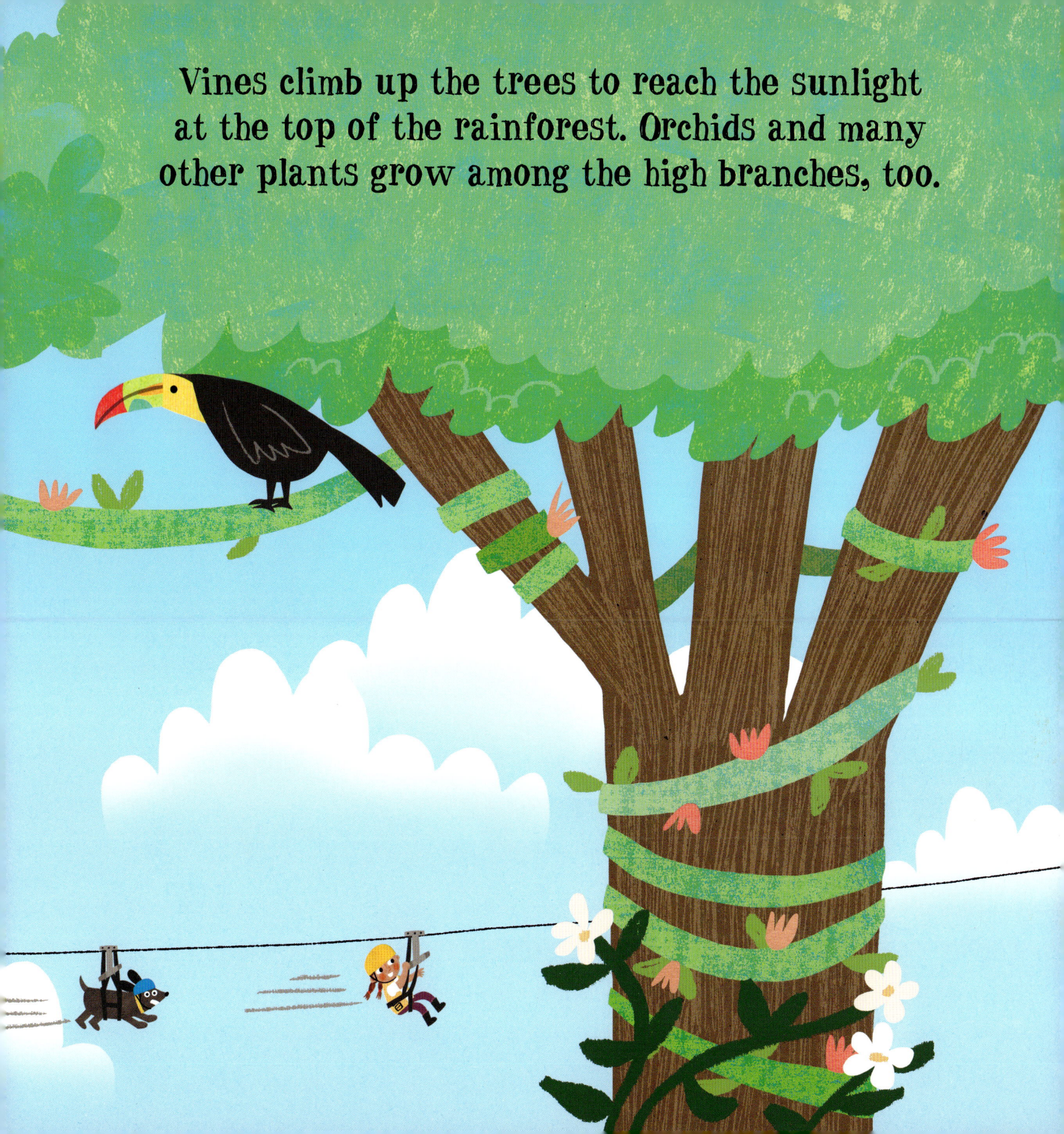

In rainforests, there are lots of plants.
But there is little room to grow, so these
plants have to work hard to survive.

Some plants use special chemicals to scare away insect enemies. These chemicals are very useful for humans too. They can also be used to make medicines!

Kingfishers, macaws, toucans, parrots
and hornbills live in the rainforest.
These colourful birds fly among the treetops.

The harpy eagle lives in the rainforest too.
One of the largest birds of prey in the world,
its wings measure up to two metres wide.

In the rainforest, monkeys, chimpanzees and orangutans leap among the trees. Meanwhile, sloths move from branch to branch very, very slowly.

Far below, larger
animals like tigers, jaguars,
leopards and gorillas roam through
different rainforests around the world.

So much rain falls that huge rivers run through rainforests. The Amazon river flows through the Amazon rainforest.

Here, there are piranhas – fish with very sharp teeth. Electric eels shock their victims! Meanwhile, crocodiles, caimans and anacondas lurk in the water, watching out for prey ...

Some of the trees in the Amazon rainforest are one thousand years old. But did you know that rainforests have been around for much, much longer?

There have been rainforests on Earth for millions of years. Scientists think they may be even older than the dinosaurs!

Every year, rainforest trees are cut down to make room for houses, mines and farms. This is called deforestation. The timber is used as fuel. It is also used to make paper, furniture and new homes.

Deforestation means
that rainforest species
struggle to survive.
It may cause drought
and floods.

But now people are trying to stop deforestation.
They are also planting new trees. We can help by using
less paper and recycling more.

If everyone learns how important rainforests are,
experts hope they can be saved.

THINGS TO DO

1. Paint your own rainforest, hiding as many rainforest animals as you can among the trees.

2. Many species in the rainforest are yet to be discovered, so invent your own animal. Go wild! Make it as colourful and amazing as you can!

3. Make a rainforest word cloud! Start with 'RAINFOREST', then add any other words this makes you think of. Write them all down using different coloured pens. Start like this...

RAINFOREST

TREES

VINES

NOTES FOR PARENTS AND TEACHERS

This series aims to encourage children to look at and wonder about different aspects of the world in which they live. Here are more specific ideas for getting more out of this book:

1. Make a rainforest frieze on a long piece of paper. First, cover it with rainforest foliage, then ask children to cut out and colour rainforest animals. Stick these to your fabulous frieze!

2. Without looking back through this book for clues, ask children to write down as many rainforest animals as they can remember. Who's the winner?

3. Recycling helps the rainforests. How many things can children think of to recycle?

5. Have a competition to build the tallest rainforest tree, using old newspapers. Then recycle them, of course!

RAINFOREST BOOKS TO SHARE

Can You Guess What I Am? In the Rainforest
by JP Percy
(Franklin Watts, 2016)

Discover Through Craft: Rainforests
by Jillian Powell
(Franklin Watts, 2017)

Rainforests (Fact Cat Habitats series)
by Izzi Howell
(Wayland, 2016)

Rainforests (100 Facts)
by Camilla de la Bedoyere
(Miles Kelly, 2016)

The Vanishing Rainforest
by Richard Platt,
illustrated by Rupert van Wyk
(Frances Lincoln, 2007)